The Thinking TREE

www.DyslexiaGames.com

Copyright © 2014 the Thinking Tree, LLC. All rights reserved.

Dyslexia Games
Friendly Copyright Notice:

ALL DYSLEXIA GAMES, WORKSHEETS, AND MATERIALS MAY <u>NOT</u> BE SHARED, COPIED, EMAILED, OR OTHERWISE DISTRIBUTED TO ANYONE OUTSIDE YOUR HOUSEHOLD OR IMMEDIATE FAMILY (SHARING IS STEALING).

Schools, Therapy Centers and Classroom Use: Please purchase a Teacher's License for reproduction of materials.

Please refer people interested in Dyslexia Games to our website to purchase their own copy of the materials.

The Thinking Tree LLC • 617 N Swope St. • Greenfield, IN 46140 • info@dyslexiagames.com • 317-622-8852

Word Hunt 3

Look for Words Everywhere! Look on labels, signs, books, games, news papers, magazines, and on anything else with words. Each page tells you how many letters to look for. Then you need to write each word in the spaces provided.

All through this book there "Be Creative Pages" where you can spend some time doodling just for fun.

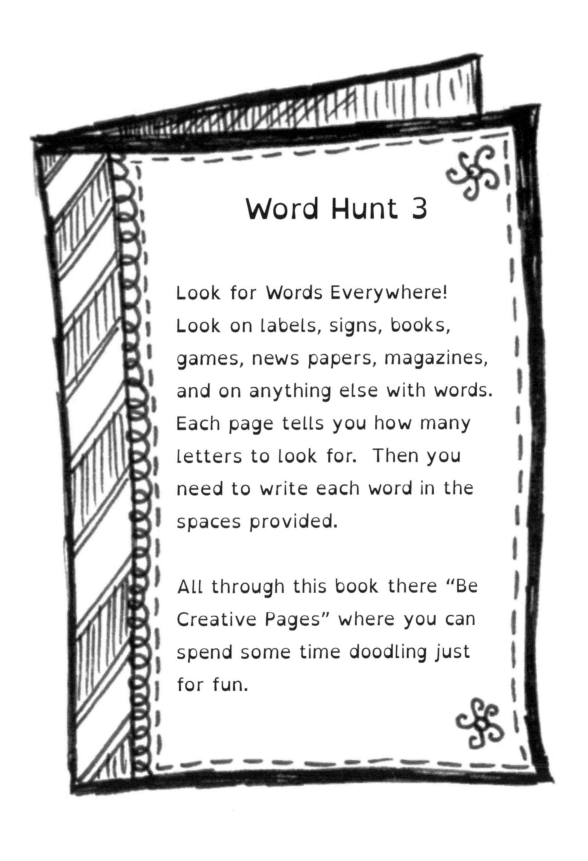

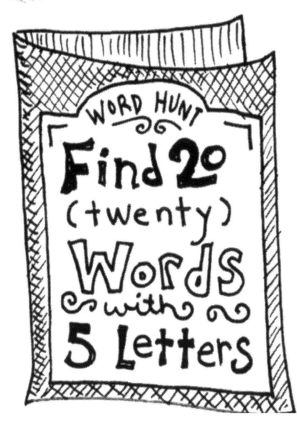
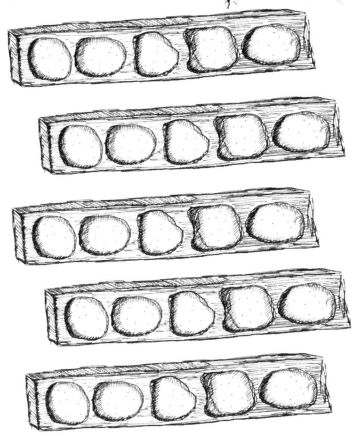

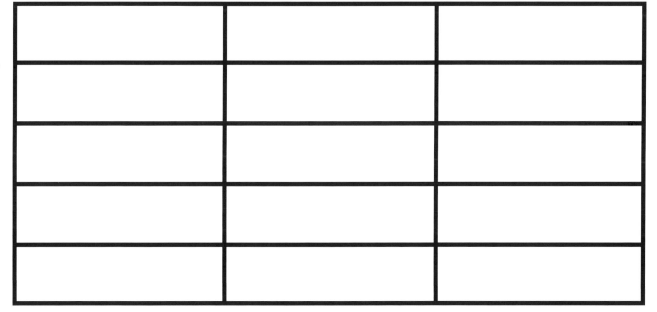

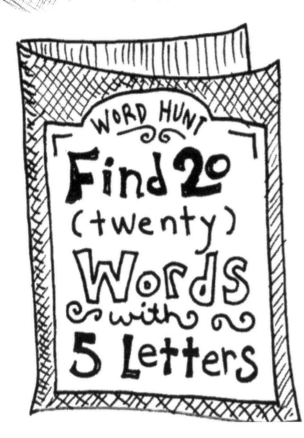
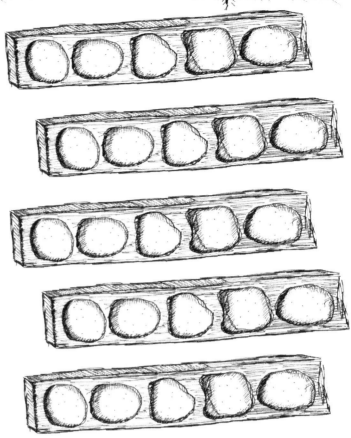

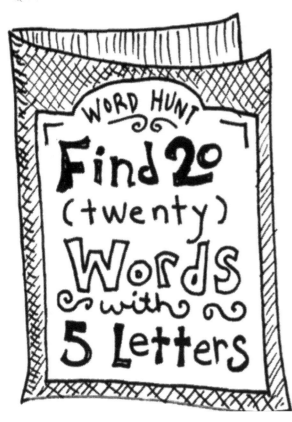
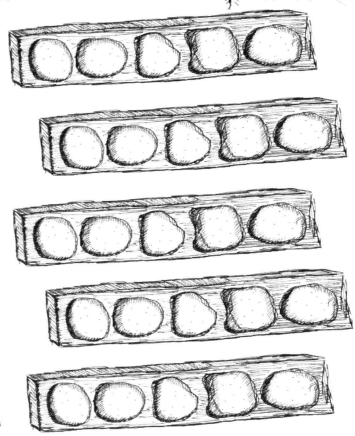
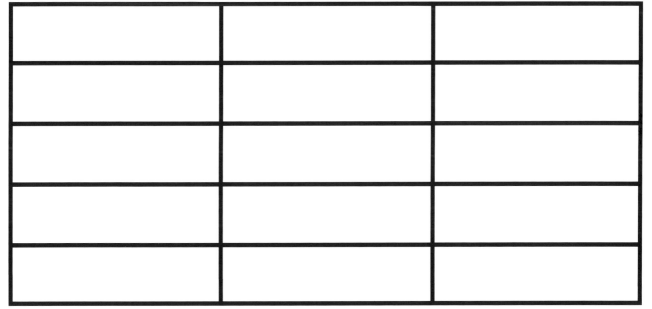

It's time to do whatever you want with this page!

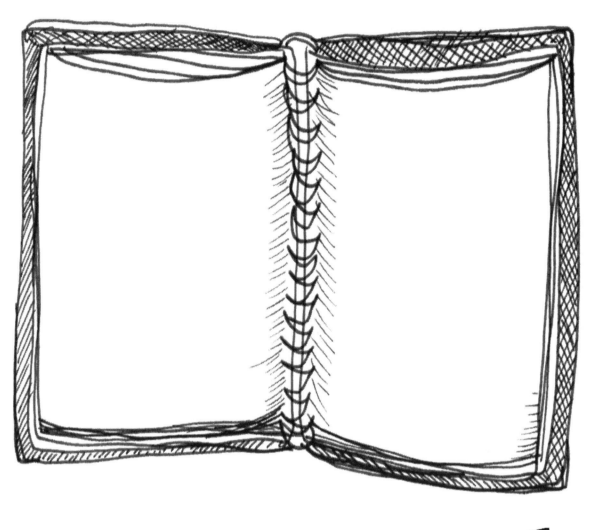

Circle ALL the FIVE Letter Words

1. absence
2. acceptable
3. accidentally
4. accommodate
5. across
6. achieve
7. acquire
8. advertise
9. advice
10. adult
11. a lot
12. almost
13. amateur
14. among
15. annually
16. apparent
17. argument
18. awful
19. balance
20. becoming
21. before
22. believe
23. breathe
24. brilliant
25. business
26. burglar
27. calendar
28. careful
29. category
30. changeable
31. citizen
32. collectible
33. column
34. coming
35. committed
36. competition
37. conscience
38. conscious
39. convenience
40. criticize
41. describe
42. decide
43. deceive
44. definite
45. definitely
46. develop
47. discipline
48. does
49. during
50. easily

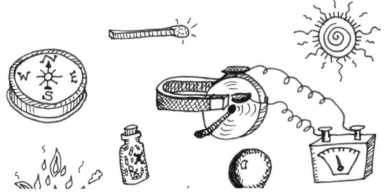

Circle ALL the SIX Letter Words

1. easily
2. eight
3. either
4. embarrass
5. equipment
6. exhilarate
7. exceed
8. excellent
9. exercise
10. existence
11. experience
12. familiar
13. finally
14. foreign
15. forty
16. friend
17. government
18. grammar
19. grateful
20. guarantee
21. happiness
22. harass
23. height
24. heroes
25. humorous
26. ignorance
27. immediate
28. independent
29. intelligence
30. interesting
31. island
32. jealous
33. jewelry
34. judgment
35. kernel
36. knowledge
37. leisure
38. lesson
39. liaison
40. liberty
41. library
42. license
43. lying
44. maintenance
45. maneuver
46. marriage
47. medieval
48. millennium
49. miniature
50. minute

Circle ALL the SIX Letter Words

1. mischievous
2. misspell
3. neighbor
4. noticeable
5. occasion
6. occasionally
7. occurrence
8. official
9. often
10. paid
11. perform
12. perseverance
13. picture
14. possession
15. precede
16. principal
17. principle
18. privilege
19. pronunciation
20. publicly
21. questionnaire
22. quiet
23. realize
24. receive
25. receipt
26. recommend
27. referred
28. reference
29. relevant
30. restaurant
31. rhyme
32. rhythm
33. safety
34. schedule
35. scissors
36. separate
37. speech
38. surprise
39. their
40. they're
41. there
42. toward
43. truly
44. twelfth
45. until
46. unusual
47. usually
48. vacuum
49. village
50. weather
51. weird

Copyright 2014 The Thinking Tree LLC - DyslexiaGames.com - Series C - Book 7

It's time to do whatever you want with this page!

Search your house and write down 30 FIVE Letter Words:

1	11	21
2	12	22
3	13	23
4	14	24
5	15	25
6	16	26
7	17	27
8	18	28
9	19	29
10	20	30

It's time to do whatever you want with this page!

It's time to do whatever you want with this page!

Circle ALL the SIX Letter Words

1. absence
2. acceptable
3. accidentally
4. accommodate
5. across
6. achieve
7. acquire
8. advertise
9. advice
10. adult
11. a lot
12. almost
13. amateur
14. among
15. annually
16. apparent
17. argument
18. awful
19. balance
20. becoming
21. before
22. believe
23. breathe
24. brilliant
25. business
26. burglar
27. calendar
28. careful
29. category
30. changeable
31. citizen
32. collectible
33. column
34. coming
35. committed
36. competition
37. conscience
38. conscious
39. convenience
40. criticize
41. describe
42. decide
43. deceive
44. definite
45. definitely
46. develop
47. discipline
48. does
49. during
50. easily

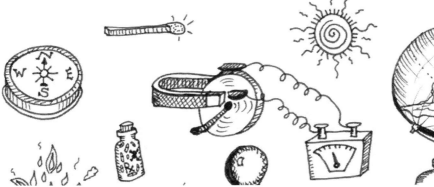

Circle ALL the SIX Letter Words

1. easily
2. eight
3. either
4. embarrass
5. equipment
6. exhilarate
7. exceed
8. excellent
9. exercise
10. existence
11. experience
12. familiar
13. finally
14. foreign
15. forty
16. friend
17. government
18. grammar
19. grateful
20. guarantee
21. happiness
22. harass
23. height
24. heroes
25. humorous
26. ignorance
27. immediate
28. independent
29. intelligence
30. interesting
31. island
32. jealous
33. jewelry
34. judgment
35. kernel
36. knowledge
37. leisure
38. lesson
39. liaison
40. liberty
41. library
42. license
43. lying
44. maintenance
45. maneuver
46. marriage
47. medieval
48. millennium
49. miniature
50. minute

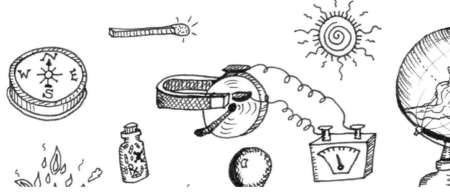

Circle ALL the SIX Letter Words

1. mischievous
2. misspell
3. neighbor
4. noticeable
5. occasion
6. occasionally
7. occurrence
8. official
9. often
10. paid
11. perform
12. perseverance
13. picture
14. possession
15. precede
16. principal
17. principle
18. privilege
19. pronunciation
20. publicly
21. questionnaire
22. quiet
23. realize
24. receive
25. receipt
26. recommend
27. referred
28. reference
29. relevant
30. restaurant
31. rhyme
32. rhythm
33. safety
34. schedule
35. scissors
36. separate
37. speech
38. surprise
39. their
40. they're
41. there
42. toward
43. truly
44. twelfth
45. until
46. unusual
47. usually
48. vacuum

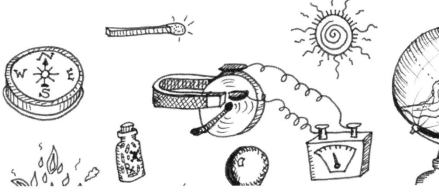

It's time to do whatever you want with this T-Shirt!

Search your House. Write down 30 SIX Letter Words:

1	11	21
2	12	22
3	13	23
4	14	24
5	15	25
6	16	26
7	17	27
8	18	28
9	19	29
10	20	30

It's time to do whatever you want with this page!

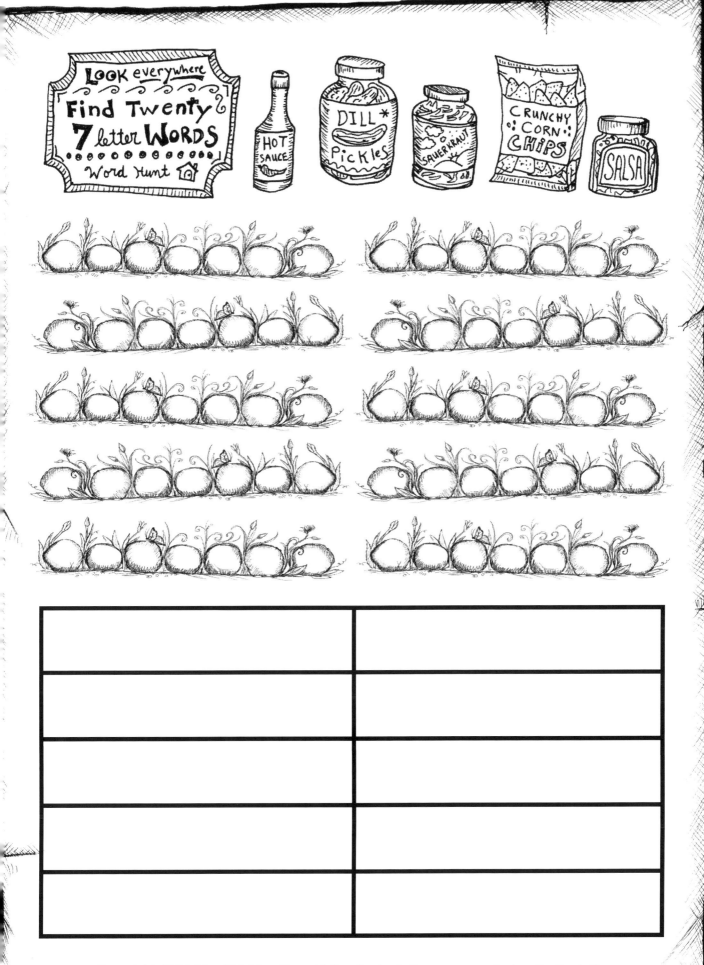

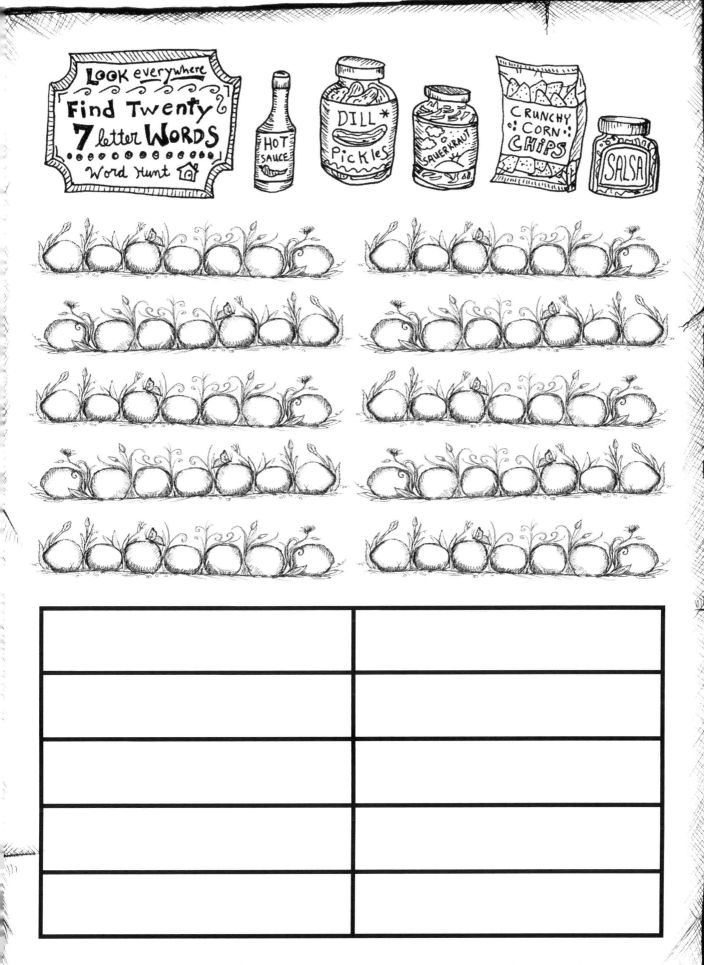

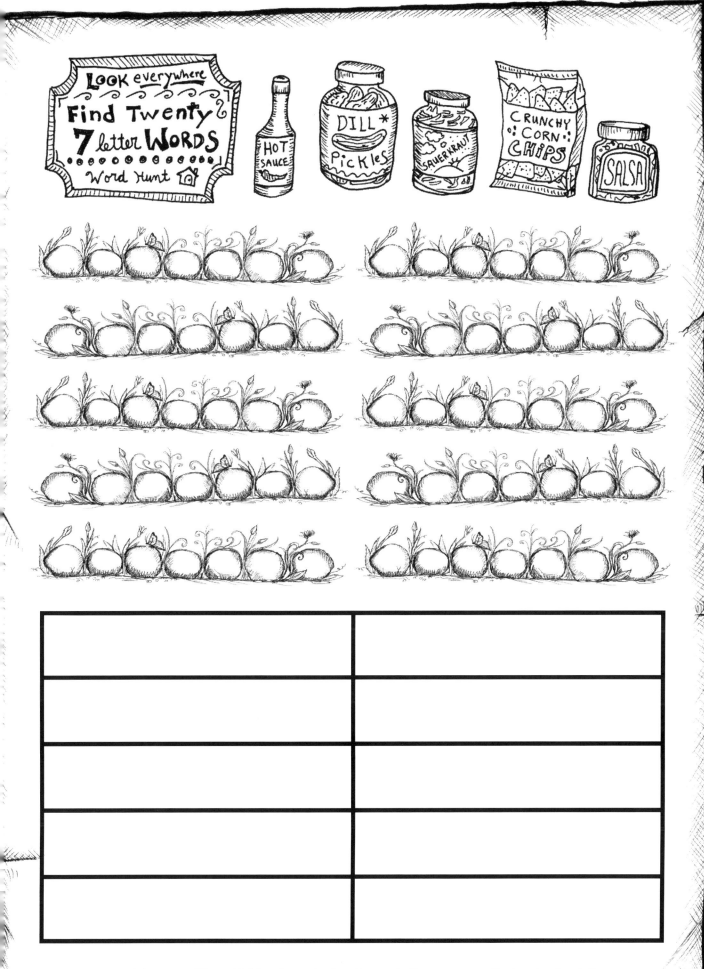

It's time to do whatever you want with this page!

Circle ALL the SEVEN Letter Words

1. absence
2. acceptable
3. accidentally
4. accommodate
5. across
6. achieve
7. acquire
8. advertise
9. advice
10. adult
11. a lot
12. almost
13. amateur
14. among
15. annually
16. apparent
17. argument
18. awful
19. balance
20. becoming
21. before
22. believe
23. breathe
24. brilliant
25. business
26. burglar
27. calendar
28. careful
29. category
30. changeable
31. citizen
32. collectible
33. column
34. coming
35. committed
36. competition
37. conscience
38. conscious
39. convenience
40. criticize
41. describe
42. decide
43. deceive
44. definite
45. definitely
46. develop
47. discipline
48. does
49. during
50. easily

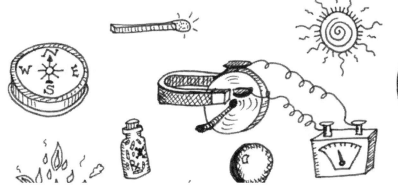

Circle ALL the SEVEN Letter Words

1. easily
2. eight
3. either
4. embarrass
5. equipment
6. exhilarate
7. exceed
8. excellent
9. exercise
10. existence
11. experience
12. familiar
13. finally
14. foreign
15. forty
16. friend
17. government
18. grammar
19. grateful
20. guarantee
21. happiness
22. harass
23. height
24. heroes
25. humorous
26. ignorance
27. immediate
28. independent
29. intelligence
30. interesting
31. island
32. jealous
33. jewelry
34. judgment
35. kernel
36. knowledge
37. leisure
38. lesson
39. liaison
40. liberty
41. library
42. license
43. lying
44. maintenance
45. maneuver
46. marriage
47. medieval
48. millennium
49. miniature
50. minute

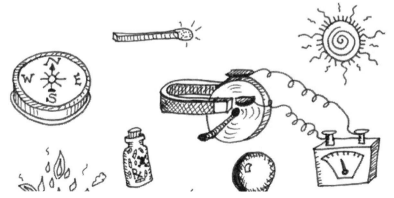

Circle ALL the SEVEN Letter Words

1. mischievous
2. misspell
3. neighbor
4. noticeable
5. occasion
6. occasionally
7. occurrence
8. official
9. often
10. paid
11. perform
12. perseverance
13. picture
14. possession
15. precede
16. principal
17. principle
18. privilege
19. pronunciation
20. publicly
21. questionnaire
22. quiet
23. realize
24. receive
25. receipt
26. recommend
27. referred
28. reference
29. relevant
30. restaurant
31. rhyme
32. rhythm
33. safety
34. schedule
35. scissors
36. separate
37. speech
38. surprise
39. their
40. they're
41. there
42. toward
43. truly
44. twelfth
45. until
46. unusual
47. usually
48. vacuum
49. village
50. weather
51. weird

Copyright 2014 The Thinking Tree LLC - DyslexiaGames.com - Series C - Book 7

It's time to do whatever you want with this page!

Search your house. Write down 30 SEVEN Letter Words:

1	11	21
2	12	22
3	13	23
4	14	24
5	15	25
6	16	26
7	17	27
8	18	28
9	19	29
10	20	30

It's time to do whatever you want with this page!

It's time to do whatever you want with this T-Shirt!

Circle ALL the EIGHT Letter Words

1. absence
2. acceptable
3. accidentally
4. accommodate
5. across
6. achieve
7. acquire
8. advertise
9. advice
10. adult
11. a lot
12. almost
13. amateur
14. among
15. annually
16. apparent
17. argument
18. awful
19. balance
20. becoming
21. before
22. believe
23. breathe
24. brilliant
25. business
26. burglar
27. calendar
28. careful
29. category
30. changeable
31. citizen
32. collectible
33. column
34. coming
35. committed
36. competition
37. conscience
38. conscious
39. convenience
40. criticize
41. describe
42. decide
43. deceive
44. definite
45. definitely
46. develop
47. discipline
48. does
49. during
50. easily

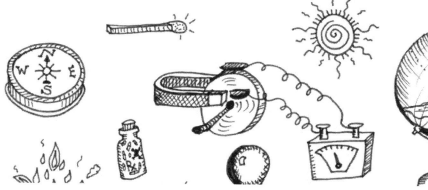

Circle ALL the EIGHT Letter Words

1. easily
2. eight
3. either
4. embarrass
5. equipment
6. exhilarate
7. exceed
8. excellent
9. exercise
10. existence
11. experience
12. familiar
13. finally
14. foreign
15. forty
16. friend
17. government
18. grammar
19. grateful
20. guarantee
21. happiness
22. harass
23. height
24. heroes
25. humorous
26. ignorance
27. immediate
28. independent
29. intelligence
30. interesting
31. island
32. jealous
33. jewelry
34. judgment
35. kernel
36. knowledge
37. leisure
38. lesson
39. liaison
40. liberty
41. library
42. license
43. lying
44. maintenance
45. maneuver
46. marriage
47. medieval
48. millennium
49. miniature
50. minute

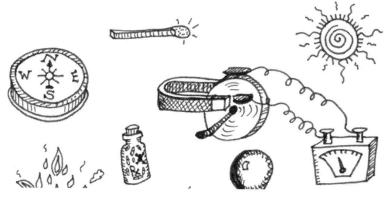

Circle ALL the EIGHT Letter Words

1. mischievous
2. misspell
3. neighbor
4. noticeable
5. occasion
6. occasionally
7. occurrence
8. official
9. often
10. paid
11. perform
12. perseverance
13. picture
14. possession
15. precede
16. principal
17. principle
18. privilege
19. pronunciation
20. publicly
21. questionnaire
22. quiet
23. realize
24. receive
25. receipt
26. recommend
27. referred
28. reference
29. relevant
30. restaurant
31. rhyme
32. rhythm
33. safety
34. schedule
35. scissors
36. separate
37. speech
38. surprise
39. their
40. they're
41. there
42. toward
43. truly
44. twelfth
45. until
46. unusual
47. usually
48. vacuum
49. village
50. weather
51. weird

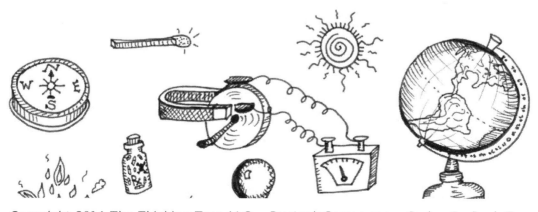

Copyright 2014 The Thinking Tree LLC - DyslexiaGames.com - Series C - Book 7

It's time to do whatever you want with this page!

Search your House. Write down 30 EIGHT Letter Words:

1	11	21
2	12	22
3	13	23
4	14	24
5	15	25
6	16	26
7	17	27
8	18	28
9	19	29
10	20	30

It's time to do whatever you want with this page!

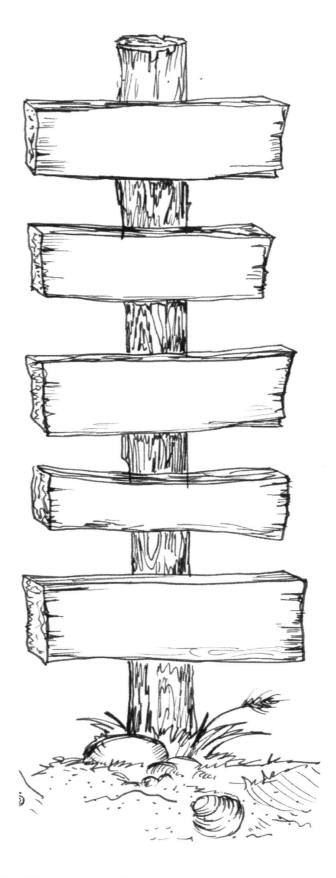

WORD HUNT 3

Practice Pages

Write down 30 THREE Letter Words:

1	11	21
2	12	22
3	13	23
4	14	24
5	15	25
6	16	26
7	17	27
8	18	28
9	19	29
10	20	30

Write down 30 FOUR Letter Words:

1	11	21
2	12	22
3	13	23
4	14	24
5	15	25
6	16	26
7	17	27
8	18	28
9	19	29
10	20	30

Write down 30 FIVE Letter Words:

1	11	21
2	12	22
3	13	23
4	14	24
5	15	25
6	16	26
7	17	27
8	18	28
9	19	29
10	20	30

Write down 30 SIX Letter Words:

1	11	21
2	12	22
3	13	23
4	14	24
5	15	25
6	16	26
7	17	27
8	18	28
9	19	29
10	20	30

Write down 30 SEVEN Letter Words:

1	11	21
2	12	22
3	13	23
4	14	24
5	15	25
6	16	26
7	17	27
8	18	28
9	19	29
10	20	30

Write down 30 NINE Letter Words:

1	11	21
2	12	22
3	13	23
4	14	24
5	15	25
6	16	26
7	17	27
8	18	28
9	19	29
10	20	30

Write down 30 TEN Letter Words:

1	11	21
2	12	22
3	13	23
4	14	24
5	15	25
6	16	26
7	17	27
8	18	28
9	19	29
10	20	30

Write down 30 ELEVEN Letter Words:

1	11	21
2	12	22
3	13	23
4	14	24
5	15	25
6	16	26
7	17	27
8	18	28
9	19	29
10	20	30

Write down 30 TWELVE Letter Words:

1	11	21
2	12	22
3	13	23
4	14	24
5	15	25
6	16	26
7	17	27
8	18	28
9	19	29
10	20	30

Write down 30 THIRTEEN Letter Words:

1	11	21
2	12	22
3	13	23
4	14	24
5	15	25
6	16	26
7	17	27
8	18	28
9	19	29
10	20	30

Write down 30 REALLY LONG Words:

1	11	21
2	12	22
3	13	23
4	14	24
5	15	25
6	16	26
7	17	27
8	18	28
9	19	29
10	20	30

It's time to do whatever you want with this page!

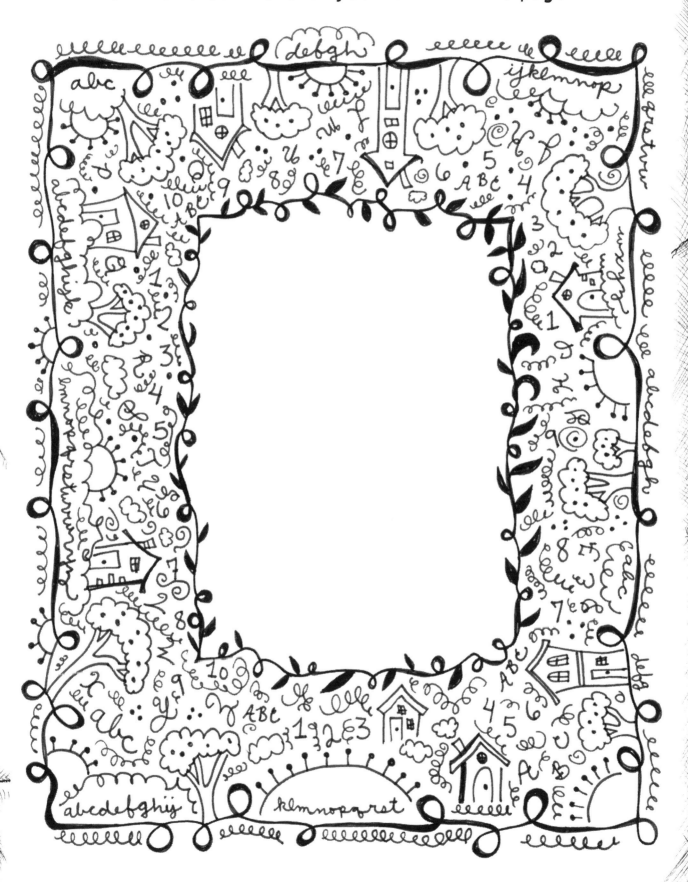

Made in the USA
Middletown, DE
04 July 2024

56749191R00064